THE
Aspiring Artist's
STUDIO

Stained
Glass

THE
Aspiring Artist's
STUDIO

Stained
Glass

Haim Raz

Sterling Publishing Co., Inc.
New York

Designed by Eddie Goldfine
Layout by Ariane Rybski
Edited by Shoshana Brickman
Photography by Matt Cohen

Library of Congress Cataloging-in-Publication Data Available

2 4 6 8 10 9 7 5 3

Published by Sterling Publishing Co., Inc.
387 Park Avenue South, New York, NY 10016
© 2007 by Penn Publishing Ltd.
Distributed in Canada by Sterling Publishing
c/o Canadian Manda Group, 165 Dufferin Street,
Toronto, Ontario, Canada M6K 3H6
Distributed in the United Kingdom by GMC Distribution Services,
Castle Place, 166 High Street, Lewes, East Sussex, England BN7 1XU
Distributed in Australia by Capricorn Link (Australia) Pty. Ltd.
P.O. Box 704, Windsor, NSW 2756, Australia

Printed in China
All rights reserved

Sterling ISBN-13: 978-1-4027-3258-4
ISBN-10: 1-4027-3258-9

For information about custom editions, special sales, premium and
corporate purchases, please contact Sterling Special Sales
Department at 800-805-5489 or specialsales@sterlingpub.com.

Introduction

Stained glass is a beautiful, ancient craft that continues to attract and intrigue artists, hobbyists, and craftspeople today. Once a complicated procedure based on difficult, often secret techniques, it is now a popular pastime that enables people to make colorful windows, vibrant lampshades, and one-of-a-kind ornaments in their home workshops.

Author and artist Haim Raz has compiled more than twenty-five of his favorite projects in *The Aspiring Artist's Studio: Stained Glass*. The projects guide readers on how to express their artistic style using various stained glass techniques. The book contains detailed guidelines, step-by-step photos and helpful patterns, as well as numerous suggestions for improvisation and adaptation. Haim also shares many helpful tips with the reader, gathered over years of experience working in the field.

The projects in this book are based on the method invented by Louis Comfort Tiffany, an American artist and glassmaker known for his innovative and beautiful stained glass creations. It is a straightforward method in which individual pieces of glass are wrapped in copper foil and soldered together using a tin alloy.

All the projects can be completed in a home workshop, using standard stained glass tools and materials. Each project is accompanied by full-color photos, and each is open to alterations, so choose the motifs, colors, and types of glass you prefer. While you may choose to follow closely the patterns for the first few projects, you will likely gain confidence as you gain experience, and be inspired to adjust and improvise as you proceed.

Haim Raz became a glass artist by profession relatively late in life. For many years, working with stained glass was a hobby he pursued only in his spare time. This enabled Haim to discover and perfect the simple techniques described in this book. "I am drawn by the charmed beauty of stained glass," Haim explains, "by its ability to transform light into something enchanting." This book is for others who are entranced by the beauty of stained glass, by its ability to transform ordinary light into magical beams that change according to location, time of day, and season.

Note from the Author

Using this book

The projects in this book are separated into several chapters. Projects in the first chapter are relatively easy; perfect if you are just starting out. Later chapters include projects that require more time and experience. I recommend first trying some of the projects in the first chapter; when you feel confident, move on to more challenging projects.

Patterns

Near the back of the book, you'll find more than twenty project patterns. Photocopy, enlarge, and adjust to suit your style. Of course, you can also follow the instructions for any project in this book using a pattern you designed, or one you have adapted from another source.

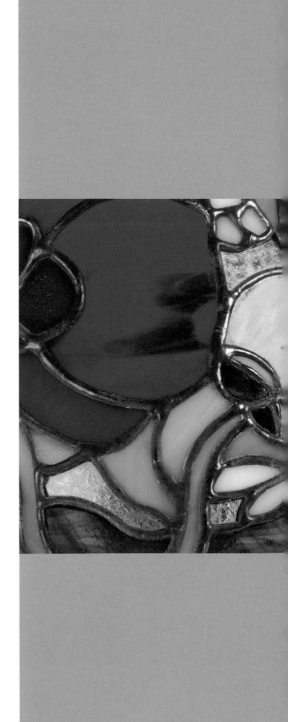

Become familiar with the materials

Carefully follow the instructions for each project, and consult with experts at your local stained glass shop if you are in doubt about any material or technique. Taking a course in stained glass at a local college or community center can also help you become more familiar with the craft.

Ask for advice

If you're vacillating about what glass to choose or what design to integrate into a project, ask others for input. Even someone who knows little about stained glass may have great ideas about design, color, or texture.

Keep your eyes open

Stained glass is a hobby that can accompany you everywhere you go. Keep a sketchbook and camera on hand when traveling for recording ideas or designs you may want to use in your work.

Unusual supplies

Be on the lookout for unique lampshades, beautiful pieces of glass, and out-of-the-ordinary molds. While standard items can always be purchased at hobby stores, surprising treasures can also be found at garage sales and flea markets.

Follow the order that works best for you

In this book, I describe the order that works best for me. You may find you prefer to work in a different order. Do whatever is most comfortable for you.

A well-planned start is the best finish

Think about all the steps in your project in advance. You may even want to write a general plan. This can help save time, money, and frustration.

Check yourself as you go

If you find a certain stage has gone awry—perhaps your sketch is too complicated, perhaps you didn't cut the glass accurately—go back and correct it. Fixing errors early on is much easier than correcting them at a later stage.

Take a photo!

Photograph every finished project—especially if you plan on giving it away. It can also be helpful to photograph stages as you go.

Acknowledgements

Thanks to my wife Azik, who has always supported me and been my best art critic. Thanks to my children Yam, Advah, Yuval, and Tal, who have provided homes for many of my projects, and given me endless encouragement. Thanks also to the editor, Shoshana Brickman, for helping me express my thoughts clearly and simply. A special thanks to Tal, who built a beautiful website for exhibiting my work.

Safety First

Working in stained glass involves electrical equipment, sharp materials, and harsh chemicals. **Exercise caution** at all times.

Read and follow the instructions on all tools and materials.

Cut glass is sharp. No matter how careful you are, you will probably cut yourself every once in a while, so keep a **well-stocked first aid kit** in your workshop.

Safety glasses should always be worn when cutting, grinding, and soldering.

Wear **work gloves** when sorting or moving large pieces of glass.

Don't break scored glass with your hands. Always use pliers.

Your Workshop

Set up your workshop in an area that is **well ventilated** and **well lit**. You may want to invest in a fume trap to absorb dangerous vapors.

Keep your workshop **tidy and organized**. This reduces the chance of accidents and cuts down on the time you spend looking for items as you work.

Store your glass in a place that is **easy to access**. Make sure it is far from your legs and arms as you work.

Cover your work surface with a **plywood board** that can support leading nails and jigs.

Keep the floor in your workroom **clean**. I recommend tile, linoleum, or wood floors, not carpet.

Stained glass tools and materials can be dangerous, so **keep small children and pets out of your workroom**.

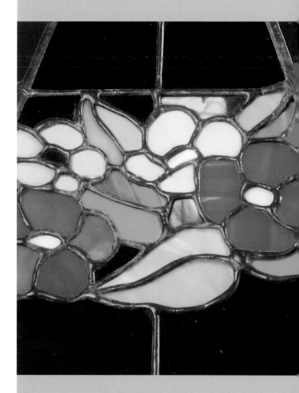

Tools and Materials

The following tools and materials can be purchased at stained glass shops and hobby stores. There are also many sources for shopping online, allowing you to order supplies straight to your door.

Although you may already have some of these tools in your home, I recommend leaving the ones you need for stained glass in your workshop permanently, so that they are always handy and available.

Tools

- **Board** to cover your work surface. A plywood board is best. It must be able to support leading nails and a jig and should be about 2 inches larger than your project.
- **Brushes** to apply flux and patina. These rust over time, so always have a few extras on hand.
- **Burnisher, fid,** or any small roll to press the copper foil onto the edges of the glass.
- **Corkbacked ruler** to score straight lines.
- **Damp cloths** to reduce heat while soldering.
- **Disposable nylon gloves** to protect your hands when applying patina.
- **Drawing materials** to make patterns. This includes a pencil, eraser, compass, ruler, white paper, and transparencies. You'll also need access to a photocopier to make copies.
- **Fume trap** to protect you from hazardous vapors.
- **Glass cutter** to score glass.
- **Glass grinder** to smooth the edges of cut glass.
- **Jig** to make frames for projects with straight edges and repeating panels.
- **Leading nails** to hold glass in place before soldering.
- **Pattern shears** for copper foiling to cut out pattern pieces. These shears remove a margin of paper as they cut, leaving a gap for the solder.

Burnisher, fid

Glass cutters

Glass grinder

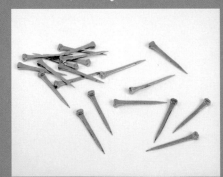

Leading nails

Pattern shears

- **Permanent markers** to mark glass.
- **Pliers** to break glass along score lines:
  - **Breaking pliers** to break long, straight pieces of glass.
  - **Grozing pliers** to trim rough edges on glass.
  - **Running pliers** to break curved or straight pieces of glass.
- **Rope** or **clamps** to bind plywood boards when turning over large projects.
- **Round-nose pliers** to bend copper wire.
- **Safety glasses** to protect your eyes when cutting, grinding, and soldering.
- **Sandpaper** to sand small pieces of glass.
- **Scissors** to cut copper foil.
- **Solder iron with stand** to melt solder. The standard tip for soldering is ¼ inch, but other tips can be used, depending upon the size of the project.
- **Wire cutters** to cut copper wire and solder.
- **Work gloves** to protect your hands when handling glass.

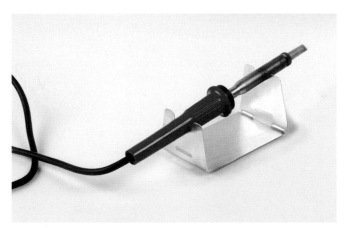

Solder iron with stand

Permanent markers

Breaking pliers

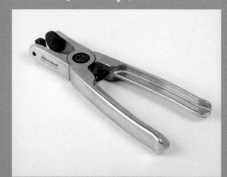

Grozing pliers

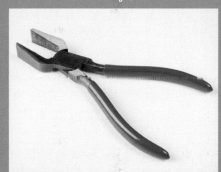

Running pliers

Round-nose pliers

Materials

- **Copper foil** to wrap glass, providing a surface for the solder to stick.
- **Copper wire** to create legs, antennae, and hooks, and provide extra support in large projects.
- **Flux** to prepare the copper foil for soldering.
- **Mirror clamps** to hold large mirrors securely in place within stained glass frames.
- **Mirror sealant** to protect mirrors from flux and patina.
- **Patina** to change the color of the solder.
- **Reinforcing strips** to add support in large projects.
- **Solder** to join the copper-wrapped pieces of glass. Solder is usually sold in **spools**, but can also be purchased in **rods**.
- **Vase caps** to add support to lampshades and provide a site for attaching lightbulbs and releasing heat.
- **Wax** to protect the finished product.
- **Wide tape** to hold lampshade panels in place before soldering.

Glass

Glass comes in a countless array of colors and styles. While choosing glass for decorative ornaments is often based on preference alone, selecting glass for windows and lampshades demands a little more consideration, as the glass you choose directly effects the function of the product.

If you are making a window, think about its orientation toward the sun. Do you want the window to minimize heat or do you want to make the most of the light that shines through? Do you want the window to increase privacy or provide a view of the outdoor landscape? If you are making a lampshade, think about its function. Do you want the lampshade to be used as a reading lamp or desk lamp, or do you want it to cast a gentle atmospheric light?

Copper foil

Copper wire

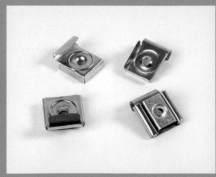

Mirror clamps

Patina

Transparency is the measure of light a glass conveys. Test the transparency of your glass by holding it up to the type of light it will transmit. If you are making a window, hold the glass up to natural sunlight; if you are making a lampshade, hold the glass up to a lightbulb.

Opalescent glass has a milky hue and transmits a gentle light. It may come in a single color, but often includes a combination of two or more colors in wisps, swirls, or spots. When used in lampshades, it may not transmit enough light for reading, but will cast a lovely glow. In windows, opalescent glass increases privacy by reducing visibility through the window; it also reduces the amount of sunlight that enters a room.

Cathedral glass transmits a stronger light. It usually comes in a single color, and is available in a wide variety of textures, such as rippled, hammered, or seedy. In lampshades, it can be quite effective for reading lamps or central light fixtures. In windows, cathedral glass allows for greater visibility through the window, and allows more rays of sunlight to penetrate into a room.

Colored glass filters some light, so consider whether you will be using dark or light colors in your project. Dark glass reduces the amount of light transmitted. In lampshades, dark glass may be appropriate for an area that doesn't require too much illumination. In windows, dark glass increases privacy and reduces the amount of sunlight transmitted through the window.

Projects that use only **uncolored glass** can be particularly striking due to the contrast between the glass and the patina. A large amount of light can be projected by a lampshade of uncolored glass, making it suitable for a reading corner, ceiling fixture, or any other area that requires illumination. Using uncolored glass can also save you time when assembling your project, as the pattern can be marked directly onto the glass.

Reinforcing strips

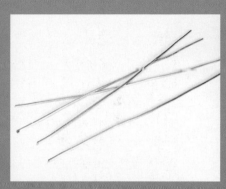

Solder rods

Solder spool

Vase caps

Basic Techniques

1 Preparing your pattern

If you are using **one of the patterns in this book**, simply photocopy and enlarge it to the appropriate size.

If you are **preparing your own pattern**, use stained glass journals, magazines, and the Internet for ideas and examples. If you are **sketching your picture freehand**, be sure that the drawing is within your capabilities. If you are new to the craft, keep the pattern relatively simple.

Assign a number to each piece in your pattern. You'll transfer these numbers to the glass before cutting it.

Mark flow lines on each piece in your pattern, and use these lines to help you orient the glass according to its natural flow.

Make a photocopy of your pattern. Cut one copy and use it to mark the glass. Lay the whole copy on your work surface to guide you in assembling the glass.

In projects that require you to reuse a pattern, photocopy the pattern onto **transparencies**. More durable than paper, transparencies can be reused several times to mark glass.

2 Selecting the glass

Transparency, **color**, and **texture** are important considerations when choosing glass. For more information, see Glass (pages 16–17).

The amount of glass you use depends upon the flow of glass, the shape of your pieces, and the accuracy of your cutting. There is nothing more frustrating than running out of a specific glass before finishing a project, so **always buy about 25% more than you think you need for a specific project.**

Tip: If you are cutting several pieces from a large sheet of glass, cut the glass into smaller sections before you start. This will make it easier to handle as you work.

3 Marking the glass

Use a **permanent marker** to mark glass.

Keep in mind that most glass has a **smooth side** and a **rough side**. It is easier to cut glass on the smooth side, but either side can be used for the front of a project. The amount of light transmitted from both sides of the glass is equal.

Be precise when marking glass, and make sure the pattern is steady as you mark. Use a **cork-backed ruler** for marking straight lines.

Transfer the numbers from your pattern onto the glass. This will help you assemble the pieces later.

For **symmetrical objects** such as butterfly wings, use the same pattern to mark both sides, just flip it over.

Tip: Mark pieces to be cut from the same glass, particularly those that appear side by side in your project, at the same time. This will save you cutting time and reduce the amount of wasted glass.

4 Cutting the glass

Always wear **safety glasses** when scoring, breaking, and grinding glass.

Scoring

Carefully **follow the instructions** of your glass cutting tool and ensure that the cutting wheel is sufficiently oiled.

Place the glass **flat** on your work surface. If possible, cover the work surface with a cloth to prevent the glass from slipping as you cut.

Score the glass on the **inside of the marked line**, so that the piece you cut is as clean as possible.

Be sensitive to the pressure you use to score the glass. Too much pressure will wear down your glass cutter; too little pressure will make a score that is too shallow.

Use a **cork-backed ruler** to score straight lines.

Tip: *The more accurately you score the glass, the less grinding you'll have to do later to make the glass the right size.*

Cutting Curves

Curves should be scored gradually. First mark and score the curve you want to achieve. Then score a series of smaller curves. Remove the smaller curves one at a time until you reach the curve you want.

Cutting Circles

Circles should be scored in sections. First mark the circle on a piece of glass, making sure there is a margin on all sides. Score the circumference of the circle in sections and break off each section as you go. If you only need a small circle for your project, consider using a nugget instead of cut glass.

Breaking

Use pliers to break all pieces of glass. Use **breaking pliers** to break long, straight pieces of glass and **running pliers** to break curved or straight pieces of glass. **Grozing pliers** are helpful for trimming rough edges of glass.

Hold the glass with the pliers and gently tap on either side of the score line. You'll know the glass has separated along the score line when you **hear a soft click**. Apply more pressure to the pliers to separate the pieces completely.

Pliers may not be helpful for breaking larger pieces of glass. In such cases, hold the glass near your work surface and **gently tap the underside**

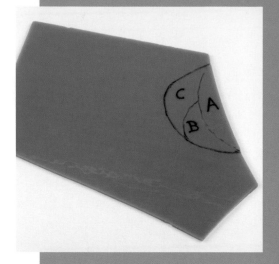

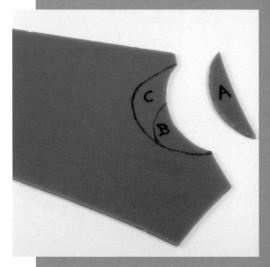

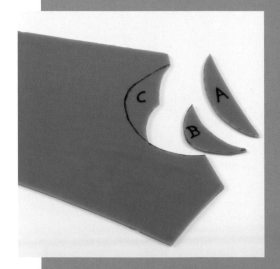

directly under the score line. Many glass cutters have a ball on one end specifically for this purpose. Be sure to keep the glass close to your work surface as you tap, in case it breaks suddenly. Do not break glass over your knees or at a distance from the floor.

Tip: Clean your work surface with a brush after each piece of glass you cut as small pieces of glass may be left behind after breaking the glass. These can scratch the next piece of glass or cut your hands. Never clean your work surface with your hands.

Grinding

After the glass is cut, the edges will be sharp and jagged. Grinding **smoothes the edges of the glass**, providing an even surface for the copper foil to stick. Jagged edges aren't just dangerous; they can also rip the copper foil. If you are using glass nuggets, grind the nuggets around the center as this makes it easier for the copper foil to stick.

I recommend using an **electric glass grinder** for most pieces of glass. You can use **sandpaper** to grind particularly small pieces of glass, although this can be very time-consuming.

Hold the glass firmly as you grind. This is especially important when grinding small pieces of glass or nuggets.

Be sensitive to the amount of pressure you apply when holding the glass against the grinder. Newer grinder bits require less pressure, whereas older ones may require more pressure.

Take extra care when **grinding mirrors**, as too much pressure can cause the mirror to chip. Use a duller bit on your grinder or use a **mirror grinding bit** designed especially for this purpose.

Wash the glass with soap and water after grinding to remove dust and oil residue. Dry thoroughly with a soft cloth.

Arrange the pieces of glass onto the whole pattern to make sure they fit. If necessary, grind again to make adjustments.

5 Applying copper foil

Copper foil provides the surface onto which the solder sticks. It is a thin sheet of copper with a sticky side that adheres to the glass; the other side receives the solder. The sticky side of the copper foil may be visible in the final product, so choose a color that suits your design. Standard copper foil is **copper backed**. There is also **black-backed copper foil** and **silver-backed copper foil**, both popular choices when working with mirror or transparent glass.

Copper foil comes in **various widths**; choose the width of your foil according to the thickness of your glass. The foil must cover the edge of the glass and leave an **even margin on either side of the glass.**

Applying copper foil

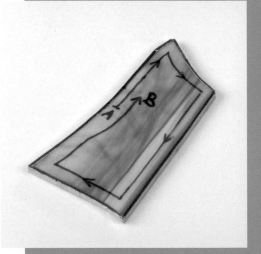

Start wrapping the copper foil in an area of the glass that will be **flush with another piece of glass**. This reduces the chance that the foil will separate from the glass during soldering. When wrapping nuggets, place the foil around the center of the nugget.

Allow the copper foil to **overlap by about ¼ inch** then cut with a scissors. **Burnish** the copper foil along the edge and margins using a burnisher, fid, or any small roll that is comfortable to hold.

Tip: Copper foil oxidizes over time, inhibiting the solder process. When working on large projects, I recommend covering the pieces of glass with a thin layer of solder after wrapping them in copper foil. This protects the foil from oxidization and makes soldering the pieces together later much easier. Keeping wrapped pieces of glass in the refrigerator also helps slow down the oxidization process (although this may interfere with your cooking).

6 Soldering

Place the whole pattern on your work surface.
If you are using a jig, nail pieces of wood along the edges of the pattern. Leave a corner of the jig open, so it is easier to insert the final pieces of glass.

Arrange the wrapped pieces of glass over the pattern and use leading nails to hold the pieces in place. Brush flux on places where two pieces of glass meet; I recommend using **water-soluble flux**, as its residue is easy to remove with soap and water. Use **mirror flux** when working with mirrors. In the meantime, **heat the solder iron**.

The first stage of soldering is **tack soldering**. It involves placing small dabs of solder in key joints along seams between two pieces of glass.

If you are working on a small project and the pieces are secure after tack soldering, turn over the project and solder the second side. By turning it over at this stage, you can make sure that your work is flat and evenly soldered. Lay a damp cloth under the project as you work on the second side to cool the solder so it doesn't leak through. Brush flux and tin solder the second side by applying a thin layer of solder along the seams. Turn over the project again, brush flux, and bead solder.

If your project is too large to turn over after tack soldering the first side, tin solder the first side completely before turning it over onto a damp cloth. Tin solder the second side, turn over the project again, fix up any places where the solder has leaked, and bead solder.

After bead soldering the front of the project, apply a thin layer of solder **along the edges**. To do this, lay the project on one edge and hold it upright with your hands. You may need to wear work gloves, as the glass may be warm. Soldering the edges at this stage adds support and protects the copper foil from breaking. If this piece is not going to be soldered to other pieces, brush flux along the edges and bead solder.

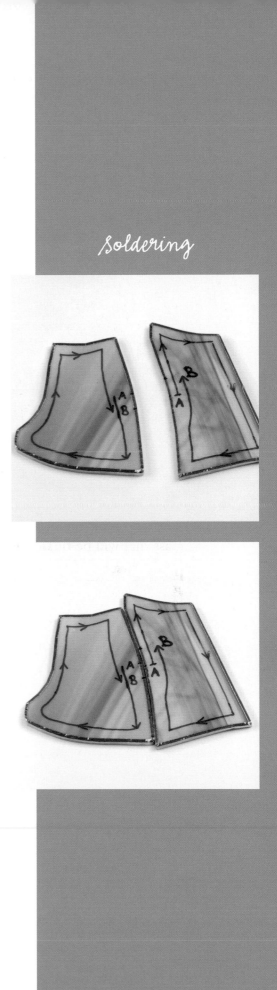

Soldering

Soldering Tips

- *If you notice that solder is dripping through to the other side of your project as you work, **place a damp cloth under the glass**. This will help cool the solder and reduce the amount that seeps through.*
- *When soldering together pieces of glass, use the **wider side** of the solder iron to produce the largest amount of heat. When soldering edges, turn the solder iron so that the **narrower side** of the solder iron is closest to the solder.*
- *Soldering doesn't just plug the space between the pieces of glass. It also **supports the glass from both sides**, creating an H-shaped frame on which the glass pieces rest.*
- *Melted solder is a **hot liquid**. Take care that it doesn't drip onto your skin or clothes.*
- *When **fixing soldered seams**, use lots of flux so that the repair blends in naturally with the original solder.*
- *To **remove solder**, gently heat the solder with the solder iron until it comes away from the seam naturally.*

7 Finishing touches

Patina changes the color of soldered seams. It comes in various colors, including black, copper, and brass. Choose a patina that complements your copper foil.

Always wear **disposable nylon gloves** and **safety glasses** when applying patina.

For a **darker finish**, apply the patina before you wash the project, while the solder is still warm. For a **lighter finish**, wash and dry your project before applying the patina.

Patina is corrosive so wash your brush carefully after applying.

8 *Cleaning up*

Clean your project as soon as possible after finishing to remove flux and oil residue.

Warm water and soap are usually good enough for cleaning, but you can also use special **stained glass cleaning products.**

If possible, let the project **soak in water** for a few hours, then scrub to remove dirt and residue.

Dry thoroughly after cleaning with a soft cloth.

Apply **stained glass finishing wax** or **high-quality car wax** to protect the seams and leave a shiny finish.

Decorative and Ornamental

These projects are great for beginning your discovery of the world of stained glass. They are fairly easy to complete and make excellent gifts for family and friends. Don't think these projects are only for beginners, though. The simple requirements mean there is lots of room for your imagination to play.

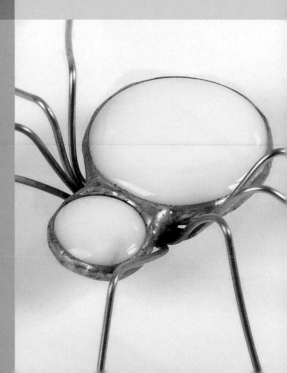

Butterfly at Rest

This is an excellent first project, as the techniques are easy and open to limitless alternatives. Feel free to experiment with wing shapes and colors, as well as the design of the body. You can follow these basic steps to make other creatures as well. Just follow the patterns on pages 113 and 114 to make crabs, dolphins, or sea turtles.

Materials

This butterfly uses two pieces of red glass for each wing. The body is made of a small and large red nugget, plus a piece of dark red glass. You'll also need 20-gauge copper wire for the antennae and ring.

Instructions

1 Photocopy the pattern (page 112) or draw your own pattern. If you are drawing your own pattern, use a single pattern for both wings. Mark it on a transparency and simply copy the reverse side to make the second wing.

2 Number the pieces and mark the flow of glass. Photocopy and cut out one of the copies (Figure A). Again, you can use a single cut pattern to mark both wings; just turn over the pieces to mark the second wing.

3 Mark and cut the glass for both wings (Figure B). Grind the nuggets around the center. Wash all of the pieces of glass and the nuggets and dry thoroughly (Figure C).

(continued on page 30)

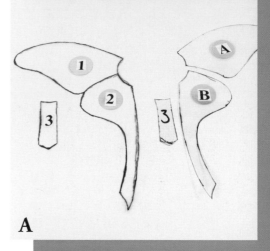

A

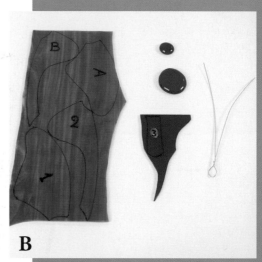

B

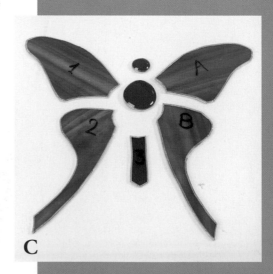

C

*A bright red butterfly brightens up
any desktop or dresser.*

4 Place the whole pattern on your work surface and lay all of the pieces to make sure they fit. Grind to make any adjustments.

5 Wrap the glass pieces and nuggets in copper foil and lay over the pattern. Use leading nails to hold the pieces in place (Figure D). Brush flux and tack solder key points. Turn over and tin solder the other side. Turn back over so that the front is facing upwards and bead solder the seams. Carefully hold the butterfly and bead solder the edges.

6 To make the antennae, cut a 12-inch piece of 20-gauge copper wire and bend in half. Form a 1-inch ring at the folded end of the wire and twist the wire a few times to secure.

7 Turn over the butterfly so that the back is facing upwards. Solder the antennae onto the seam between the two nuggets, so that the ring faces downwards and the long pieces extend upwards. Thicken the solder to stabilize. Use round-nose pliers to bend the ring upwards.

8 Turn over the butterfly so that it rests evenly on your work surface. If the antennae are too long, trim with wire cutters. Lay the antennae on a damp cloth and apply a generous amount of flux to the top of each antenna. Make a bead of solder for the rounded tip.

9 Apply patina. Wash well with soap and water and dry thoroughly.

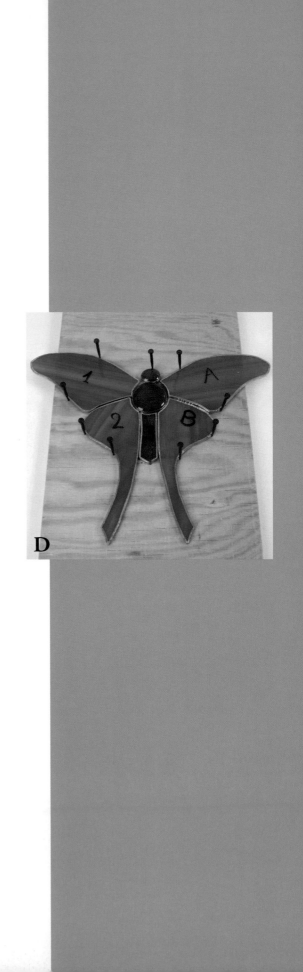

D

*Use your imagination to create various
butterfly poses and designs.*

Decorated Glass Vessel

This project is particularly easy to make due to the handiness of its main component—a broken glass vessel. The decorated container can be used to hold paintbrushes, pencils, or fresh flowers.

Materials

Wine glasses, water glasses, vases, pitchers, large bowls, or any other broken glass vessels can serve as a base for this project. Use a variety of colored glass or nuggets to make the adornment.

Instructions

1 Photocopy the pattern (page 115) or draw your own pattern.

2 Number the pieces and mark the flow of glass (Figure A). Photocopy and cut out one of the copies.

3 Mark and cut the glass. Grind the rim of the glass vessel, including the broken area. Make sure there are no cracks in the vessel, as these can worsen during soldering and cause the glass to break. Wash all of the pieces of glass and dry thoroughly.

4 Place the whole pattern on your work surface and lay the cut pieces of glass over the pattern to make sure they fit. Grind to make any adjustments.

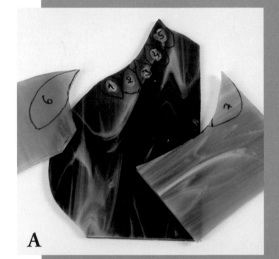

A

(continued on page 34)

Turn a cracked glass into a lovely home accessory.

5 Wrap the pieces in copper foil. Wrap the edge of the glass vessel in copper foil as well, taking care to start (and finish) in a place where the adornment will be soldered. This will strengthen the solder, and give the project a tidier finish.

Tip: If the glass vessel you are working on is made from particularly thick glass, wrap it in wider copper foil, and be sure to start wrapping from the exterior edge of the glass. If you start from the interior edge, the foil may rip when you press it around the exterior of the glass.

6 Lay the pieces that make up the flower on the pattern again; don't lay the leaves, as they will be soldered separately. Brush flux and tack solder key points. Turn over and tin solder the other side. Turn back over and bead solder the seams (Figure B).

7 Hold the adornment onto the rim and solder into place (Figure C). Solder the leaves on either side of the flower. Bead solder the edges of the leaves and flower, and around the rim of the glass vessel.

8 Apply patina. Wash well with soap and water and dry thoroughly.

Tip: You can also assemble the adornment piece by piece onto the broken glass vessel. This may be easiest if the adornment has many pieces, or if it extends across a wide area of the vessel.

B

C

Use your imagination to create containers of various sizes and styles using different types of glass vessels.

Three-Petal Coaster

Make a set of coasters for cups or a single coaster for a special vase. You can also make several coasters as mementos for a special occasion. Adjust the size of the coaster and the adornment to suit your occasion.

Materials

Use any type of glass for the coaster base and a combination of colored glass and nuggets to make the flower.

Instructions

1 Photocopy the pattern (page 116) or draw your own pattern. If you are drawing your own pattern, try to keep the adornment proportional to the base.

2 Number the pieces, mark the flow of the glass, and cut out the pieces (Figure A). There is no need to photocopy the pattern, as the flower is assembled directly onto the coaster.

3 Mark and cut the glass (Figure B). Grind the nugget around the center. Wash all of the pieces of glass and dry thoroughly.

(continued on page 38)

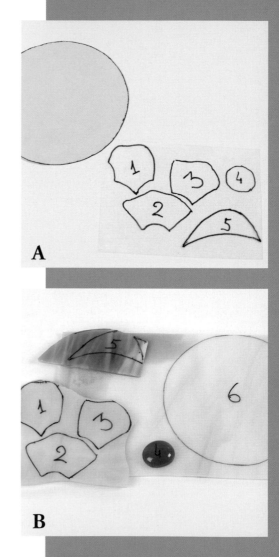

A

B

Delicate glass coasters are both functional and beautiful.

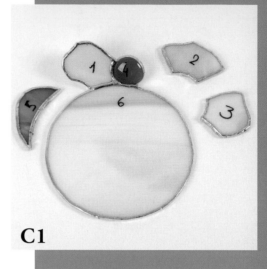

C1

4 Wrap the glass pieces and nugget in copper foil. Brush flux and solder the nugget onto the edge of the base at a gentle angle outwards. Solder one of the lower petals onto the glass nugget. Solder the other lower petal onto the nugget and then the top petal. Solder on the leaf between one of the lower petals and the base (Figures C1–3).

5 Bead solder the edges of the flower and leaf, and around the base.

6 Apply patina. Wash well with soap and water and dry thoroughly.

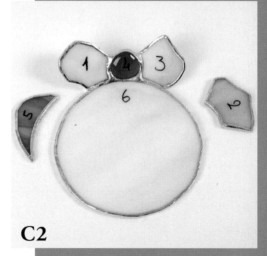

C2

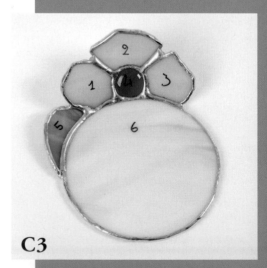

C3

Make a variety of coasters using different combinations of glass and nuggets.

Waterspout Spider

This decorative spider can be hung on a wall or placed on a table. Several spiders in different sizes and colors make a lively composition. Clearly, this project is not for people with arachnophobia!

Materials

You'll need one large nugget and one medium nugget for each spider. You'll also need four pieces of 18-gauge copper wire for the legs and one piece of 20-gauge copper wire for the ring (Figure A).

Instructions

1 Grind the nuggets around the center. Wash and dry thoroughly.

2 Wrap copper foil around the center of the nuggets. Mark where the foil overlaps on each nugget—this is the spot where you'll solder the nuggets together.

3 Brush flux and place the nuggets side by side with the flat side facing downwards. Solder together to form the body of the spider. Apply solder around each nugget and thicken the solder between the two nuggets.

4 To make the legs, cut four pieces of 18-gauge copper wire in the following lengths: 7½ inches, 6½ inches, 8 inches, and 8½ inches.

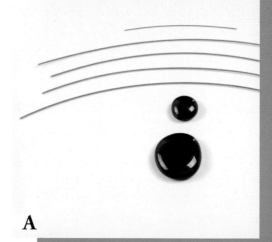

A

(continued on page 42)

This blue spider resembles a friendly daddy longlegs.

5 Mark the middle of each piece of wire. Wrap together at the middle with copper foil and solder. Cut a 4-inch piece of copper wire, bend it into a 1-inch ring, and twist the wire a few times to secure (Figure B).

6 Turn over the spider so that the flat sides of the nuggets are facing upwards. Solder the four pieces of wire to the joint between the two nuggets. Solder the hook onto the same area so that the ring is behind the smaller nugget. Thicken the solder to secure.

7 Turn over the spider so that it rests flatly on your work surface. To shape the legs, use round-nose pliers to bend each group of wires upwards (Figure C). Make sure that the angle on each side of the body is even and spread out the wires. Now bend each wire downwards to make knees and feet. Test the bends as you go to make sure the spider rests evenly on a flat surface (Figure D).

8 Apply patina. Wash well with soap and water and dry thoroughly.

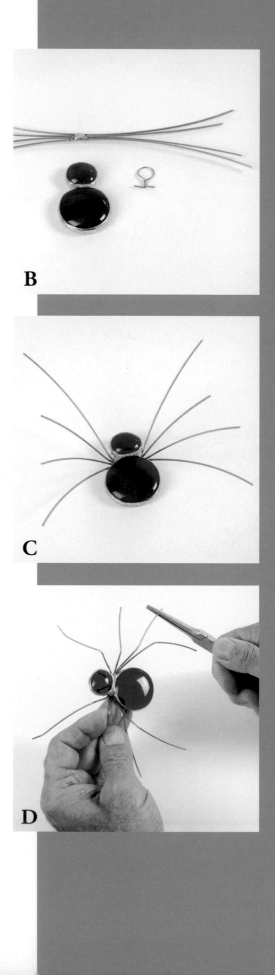

B

C

D

Create a vibrant family of spiders using
a range of brightly colored nuggets.

Butterfly—Ready for Flight

It's no surprise that artists love to create butterflies. They are among nature's most colorful creatures and offer plenty of opportunity for artistic expression. These glass butterflies add a delicate beauty to every environment.

Materials

This butterfly uses two shades of blue glass in each wing. The body is made from one medium and three small blue nuggets. You'll also need 18-gauge copper wire for the legs and 20-gauge copper wire for the antennae and ring.

Instructions

1 Photocopy the pattern (page 117) or draw your own pattern. If you are drawing your own pattern, use a single pattern for both wings. Mark one wing on a transparency and copy the reverse side to make the other wing.

2 Number the pieces and mark the flow of glass. Photocopy and cut out one of the copies (Figure A). Again, you can use a single cut pattern to mark the glass for both wings; just turn over the pieces to mark the second wing.

3 Mark and cut the glass. Grind the nuggets around the center. Wash all of the pieces of glass and the nuggets and dry thoroughly (Figure B).

4 Lay all of the pieces of glass on your work surface to make sure they fit. Use leading nails to hold the pieces in place (Figure C).

5 Grind to make any adjustments then wrap all of the pieces in copper foil. Wrap copper foil around the center of the nuggets, marking where the foil overlaps on each nugget. This is the spot where you'll solder the nuggets together.

(continued on page 46)

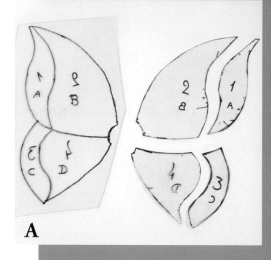

A

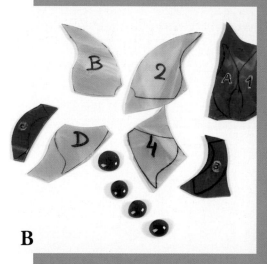

B

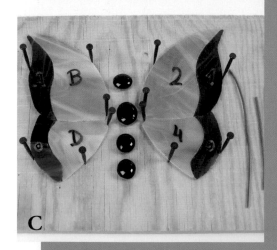

C

This butterfly includes blue, turquoise, and aquamarine glass.

6 Lay the pieces for one wing over the pattern. Brush flux and tack solder key points. Turn over and tin solder the other side. Turn back over and bead solder the seams. Carefully hold the wing and bead solder the edges.

7 To make the second wing, turn over the pattern and repeat step 6.

8 Place the medium nugget with the flat side on your work surface. Brush flux and solder on one of the wings so that it is at an angle upward. Place a cloth or small box under the wing for support.

9 Position the other wing onto the other side of the nugget, taking care to leave enough space between the two wings for attaching nuggets to the top and bottom. Solder on the second wing at the same angle as the first wing.

Tip: This is the most delicate stage in assembling the butterfly, and too much pressure on the wings could cause the foil to tear. After soldering the first wing, you may find it easier to turn over the nugget so that the flat side is facing upwards and then solder the second wing at a downward angle.

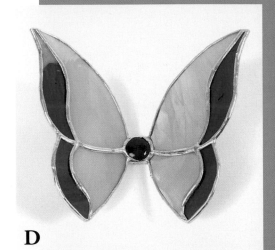

D

10 When both wings are at equal angles, bead solder them to the nugget (Figure D).

Tip: Achieving the same angle on both wings takes practice, so don't be frustrated if it takes a few tries. If the angle on both wings isn't equal, heat the solder until it comes off and solder again.

11 To make the body, position one small nugget above the medium nugget and two small nuggets below (Figure E). Make sure all of the nuggets rest evenly on your work surface, then solder them into place.

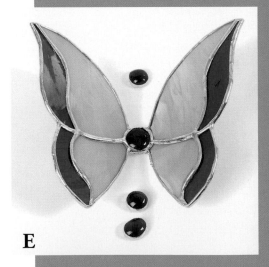

E

Tip: Although it may seem logical to solder all of the nuggets before adding the wings, I find it easier to get equal angles on the wings by first attaching them to a single nugget.

(continued on page 48)

Use clear, textured, or streakrd glass
for a variety of effects.

12 To make the legs, cut three pieces of 18-gauge copper wire in the following lengths: 4 inches, 3 inches, and 5 inches.

13 Mark the middle of each piece of wire. Wrap together at the middle with copper foil and solder together.

14 To make the antennae, cut a 12-inch piece of 20-gauge copper wire and bend in half. Form a 1-inch ring at the folded end of the wire by twisting the wire a few times.

15 Turn over the butterfly so that the flat sides of the nuggets are facing upwards. If necessary, use cloths or small boxes to support the wings. Solder on the legs at the connection between the head and the body nugget. Solder on the antennae at the same spot, so that the ring faces downwards and the long pieces extend upwards, past the head of the butterfly (Figure E). Thicken the solder to secure.

16 Turn over the butterfly so that it rests evenly on your work surface. If the antennae are too long, trim with wire cutters. Lay the antennae on a damp cloth and apply a generous amount of flux to the top of each antenna. Make a bead of solder for the rounded tip.

17 To shape the legs, use the round-nose pliers to bend each group of wires upwards, making sure that the angle on either side of the body is even (Figure F). Spread out the wires and bend each leg downwards to make knees and feet. Test the bends as you go to make sure the butterfly rests evenly on a flat surface. Bend the ring so that it faces upwards (Figure G).

18 Apply patina. Wash well with soap and water and dry thoroughly (Figure H).

F

G

H

Both simple and elaborate designs can make beautiful butterflies.

Tabletop Picture Frame

Tired of searching for the perfect frame to match a specific photograph? Your problems are solved with this versatile design.

Materials

The center of this project requires a piece of transparent glass in the size and shape of your photo. This frame is made with pieces of green glass and red nuggets; the base and sides are made with transparent glass. You'll also need 18-gauge copper wire to make a support for the photograph.

Instructions

1 Measure your photograph and use these dimensions to determine the area of transparent glass in your frame. You can also make the transparent area of the frame oval or round in shape; just make sure it reveals the area of the photo you want visible.

Tip: Because you are making your own pattern, feel free to choose a motif that suits your photo. A bunch of flowers, a colorful rainbow, and an assortment of nuggets are all lovely designs for picture frames.

2 You will also need to make a base for the frame. The length of the base depends upon the length and shape of the transparent glass. If the transparent glass is square or rectangular, the base must be the same length; if the transparent glass is round, the base glass must be same length as the frame. The width of the base for all frames must be one-third the height of the whole frame.

3 Number the pieces and mark the flow of glass. Photocopy and cut out one of the copies.

4 Mark and cut all of the pieces of glass. Grind the nuggets around the center. Wash all of the glass and dry thoroughly.

(continued on page 52)

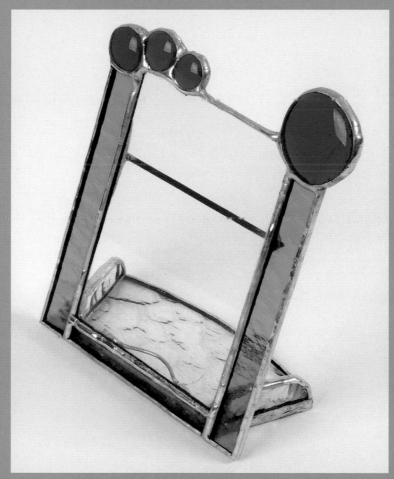

Simple frame patterns add elegance and a personal touch.

5 Place the whole pattern on your work surface and lay the glass and nuggets over the pattern to make sure they fit. Grind to make any adjustments.

6 Wrap the pieces in copper foil. Lay all of the pieces, except for the base, over the pattern. Use leading nails to hold the pieces in place (Figure A).

7 Brush flux and tack solder key points. Turn over and tin solder the other side. Turn back over and bead solder the seams. Apply a thin layer of solder to the edges of the frame.

8 To attach the base, lay the frame flat on your work surface so that the back is facing upwards. Hold the base at an angle to the frame and tack solder to the bottom of the frame. Rest the frame lightly on the base to make sure the angle is suitable, then tin solder the seam. Turn over and bead solder the other side.

Tip: You can make a cardboard model of the base and frame to determine the incline you want on the frame. Measure the angle in the model and apply to your glass frame.

9 To make the side supports, place the frame sideways on a transparency and trace the space between the base and the frame. Mark and cut two pieces of glass in this shape (Figure B). Wrap in foil and solder into place. Bead solder the edges of the frame and the base.

10 Cut a piece of 18-gauge copper wire that is the same width as the transparent glass. Place two dabs of solder on either side of the transparent glass in the top quarter of the frame. Let the dabs of solder dry, then solder the wire onto the dabs. Solder a small arc of copper wire to the center of the bottom seam of the transparent glass (Figure C).

11 Apply patina. Wash with soap and water and dry thoroughly.

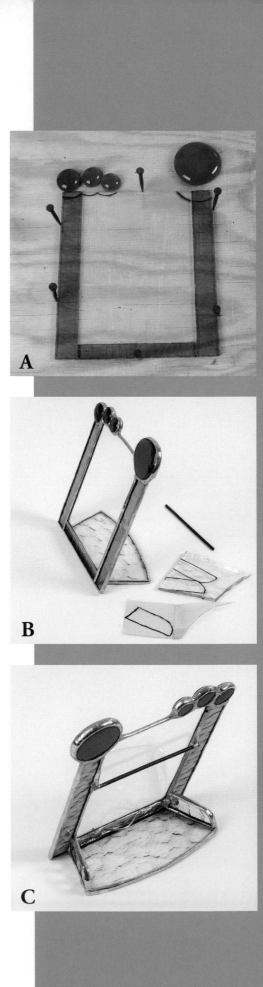

Create a variety of frames, in any dimensions, to suit every photo.

Hanging Mirror with Shelf

A large hanging mirror framed with stained glass beautifies any wall. Make an elegant frame to hang in the entrance of your home, or a playful frame to decorate a child's bedroom. Adding a small shelf onto the mirror increases its functionality and distinctness.

Materials

This project requires a large piece of mirror glass for the center and a smaller piece for the shelf. Shades of green, blue, burgundy, and orange opalescent glass are used to make the flowers and leaves. If you are making a large mirror, you'll need mirror clamps as well to secure the mirror in place.

Instructions

1 Draw patterns for your frame and shelf. Be sure to include dimensions for the mirror in the center of the frame. If you are using mirror clamps, buy the clamps in advance and include their dimensions in your pattern.

2 Number the pieces for the frame and shelf and mark the flow of glass. Photocopy and cut out one of each copy.

3 Mark and cut the glass. Be careful when grinding the edges of the mirror, as too much pressure could cause the mirror to chip. Use a duller bit on your grinder or use a mirror grinding bit designed especially for this purpose.

4 Spray the back and edges of the mirror with mirror sealant to protect it from flux and patina.

(continued on page 56)

Multicolored spring flowers are beautiful in every season.

5 Place the whole patterns for the frame and the shelf on your work surface and lay the cut pieces of glass over the patterns to make sure they fit. Grind to make any adjustments, then wrap all of the pieces in black- or silver-backed copper foil.

6 Lay all of the pieces for the frame over the pattern. Be sure to include the mirror clamps too. Brush mirror flux and tack solder key points. Turn over and tin solder the other side. Turn back over and bead solder the seams. Bead solder the edges of the frame.

7 Lay all of the pieces for the shelf adornment over the pattern, and brush mirror flux and solder both sides. Bead solder the edges of the adornment.

8 Apply patina. Wash with soap and water and dry thoroughly.

Tip: The mirror and shelf in this project are installed separately. Hang the mirror on the wall using mirror clips or a mirror anchor. Install wall brackets under the mirror and lay the shelf securely on the brackets.

Hanging Mirror with Nuggets

This mirror features an abstract design of streaked brown and gray glass, interspersed with several sizes of nuggets. The techniques used to make this mirror are similar to those described in Hanging Morning with Shelf *(page 54).*

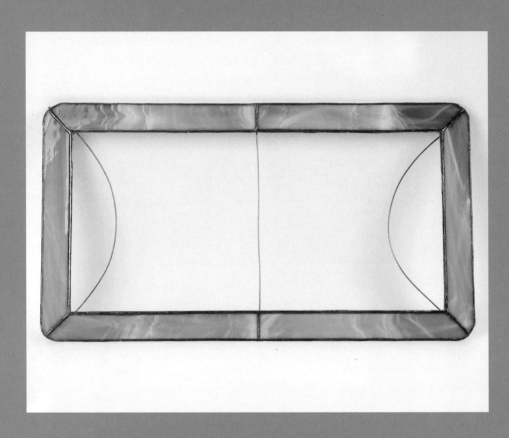

Hanging Picture Frame

To make this rectangular frame, simply follow the techniques described in Hanging Mirror with Shelf (page 54) and replace the mirror with transparent glass. Add wire supports on either side of the frame, and down the middle, to support the picture.

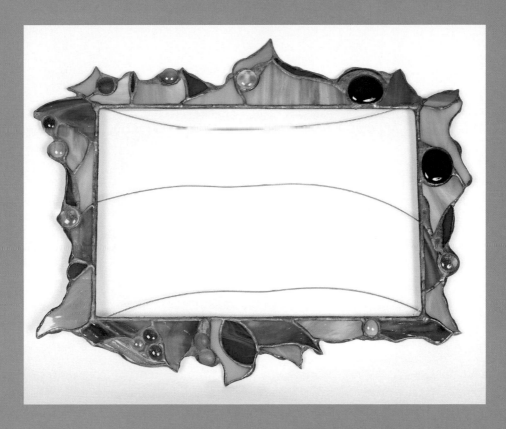

Contemporary Picture Frame

This picture frame features a striking combination of blue glass and purple nuggets, in various shades, shapes, and sizes. The techniques used in this project are similar to those described in *Hanging Mirror with Shelf* (page 54); simply replace the mirror with transparent glass and add wire support along the width of the frame to support the picture.

Windows

Stained glass windows are a beautiful addition to any home. As external features, they enhance both the inside and outside appearance. As internal room dividers, they cast a warm light throughout the house. Place your window in a spot with plenty of natural light to maximize its effect.

Planning in advance

Making a stained glass window that harmonizes with its location is the result of thoughtful planning and design. Here are some guidelines to keep in mind when designing a window to beautify your home for many years.

Size

Be very careful when measuring the space you wish to fill, as a window that is even a little too large simply won't fit. Be sure to include the size of the frame in your calculations, and double-check all measurements before finalizing your design. I recommend making the window a little smaller than necessary. The difference in a window that's a little too small can always be made up during installation, but a window that's a little too big won't fit. If possible, consult with a professional window installer to determine the exact dimensions.

Window division

When filling a large space, you must decide whether to fill it with one large window or several small windows. Making a single large window presents several challenges. Although glass seems solid, it is actually a liquid material, and an accumulation of weight and pressure on the lower part of a tall and narrow window can cause glass to crack over time. Also, large windows are very heavy, making them difficult to turn over, transport, and install.

In general, it is best to make a number of small windows to fill a large space. If you decide on a single large window, make sure the lower pieces of glass are relatively small, so that there are many copper seams to support the window's weight. Also remember that large windows require extra support, so integrate plenty of reinforcing strips to make your window stable.

Environment

There are several issues to take into consideration when it comes to environment. First, think about the inside environment of the room. Natural scenes may suit a bathroom or kitchen whereas playful scenes may be more appropriate for a child's room. It is also important to consider the environment that surrounds the room. In some cases, you may want a window that complements the outside landscape. For example, in designing a window that looks onto a garden, you may want a pattern that includes animals, birds or plants. In other cases, you may want a window that contrasts with the surroundings. For example, if you live in a city center, you may want a window with a forest or water scene to remind you of nature.

Sea of Galilee Window

*This window, situated on the balcony of my home,
complements the landscape by including colors and
objects that appear naturally in the area.*

First, I used magazines and journals to generate
an "inventory of objects" that I felt might be
suitable for the window. In making the final
selection, I considered the window's dimensions
—quite long and narrow—and chose to
incorporate long objects such as reeds that would
provide many sites for adding reinforcing strips to
support the window's weight.

The objects were first sketched separately, then
combined into a design that had the colors and
sense of movement that I wanted. After drawing
the final design, I transferred it to white paper,
drawing all of the elements in their actual size.
Due to the size of the window, I paid special
attention to the following elements:

Continuity

The seams in the background are aligned with
seams in the objects. This continuity is important
for strengthening the window.

Curved lines

Natural environments do not have many straight
lines. The curved lines in this window mimic
nature and create a sense of flow.

Vertical seams

There are many vertical seams in this window to
increase the window's strength and create a long,
elegant look.

Small pieces

There are many small pieces of glass, particularly
at the bottom of the window, to increase support
and reduce the chance that the glass will crack.

Materials

This window uses a lot of blue opalescent glass for the sea and the sky. This is set off with white and brown glass for the gulls and egrets, and several colors of glass in the kingfisher. The reeds are various shades of brown and green opalescent glass. You'll also need several reinforcing strips to make this window.

Instructions

1 Draw your window pattern to suit the dimensions of the space you wish fill. Use the patterns (pages 118–121) or draw your own patterns. Number the pieces and mark the flow of glass. Photocopy and cut out one of the copies.

2 Place a large plywood board onto your work surface. Place the whole pattern on the board and make a jig around the pattern, leaving a corner open for easy access.

3 Mark and cut the glass. I suggest cutting the pieces for each object first and laying them onto the pattern. Then cut the pieces for the background and insert them between the objects. Be sure to add several reinforcing strips, particularly in the bottom section of the window.

4 When you are satisfied with the fit of all the pieces and the quantity of reinforcing strips, remove the glass pieces, wrap in copper foil, and return to the jig. Brush flux and tack solder key points. Tin solder the whole window, making sure the solder is strong enough for turning over the window.

Tip: *Windows may take several weeks to assemble. I recommend covering copper-wrapped pieces of glass in a thin layer of solder. This protects the copper foil from oxidation and makes soldering much easier.*

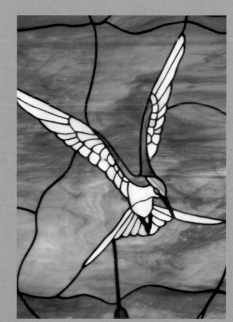

Close up view of gull in flight.

5 Spread a large damp cloth over the window and place a large plywood board over top. Secure together the two boards on either side of the glass with strong rope or clamps and carefully turn over the window.

6 Remove the top plywood board and tin solder the other side of the window. Bead solder and apply patina.

7 Wash this side of the window thoroughly with soap and water. Spread a large damp cloth over the window and make another sandwich with the plywood board. Secure with rope or clamps and carefully turn over, so that the side you worked on first is facing upwards again.

8 Remove the top plywood board and the damp cloth. Correct any small errors or leaks in the solder, then bead solder and apply patina.

9 Wash this side of the window thoroughly with soap and water. Carefully remove the damp cloth from underneath the window. I recommend having help as you do this, as it can be quite tricky. If possible, move the window to a dry, open area and allow it to dry thoroughly for a day or two.

Tip: Installing a window of this size can be quite challenging. I sandwiched it between two transparent windows, a technique that adds support and protects the window from the elements. It also makes cleaning the window much easier.

Close up view of egret.

Close up view of kingfisher.

Full view of Sea of Galilee Window

Four Fuchsia Windows

*Fuchsias are one of nature's most decorative flowers, with their
elegant shape and splendid colors. These windows are designed
to increase privacy, so they contain only opalescent glass. The
fuchsias are made from shades of purple and pink and the
leaves are made from various shades of green. The background
is milky white. The techniques used in this window are similar
to those described in Sea of Galilee Window (pages 64–66).
See page 122 for a fuchsia pattern that can help you get started.*

Purple Lace Windows

This set of windows complements the Purple Lace Lampshade
(page 94) and uses similar shades of purple and green. The
windows are situated in an exterior wall that receives a fair
share of sunlight throughout the day. The heat from these rays
can be particularly intense during the summer months,
and so I chose various shades of purple opalescent glass to reduce
the amount of light transmitted into the room. The muted light
creates a warm, intimate atmosphere. The techniques used in
this window are similar to those described in Sea of Galilee
Window (pages 64–66).
See page 123 for a lace pattern.

Indigo Morning Glory Window

Ephemeral in nature, morning glories are immensely rewarding to create in stained glass, as each flower lasts much longer than a single day. The flowers in this window are made from indigo opalescent glass. The techniques used are similar to those described in Sea of Galilee Window (pages 64–66).
See the patterns on page 124 to help you sketch the flowers and leaves.

Set of Scarlet Window

*The scarlet glass used to make the morning glories in this set of
windows casts a beautiful warm light. Like their natural
inspiration, the color in these flowers is particularly radiant
during the early morning sunlight. The techniques used are
similar to those described in* Sea of Galilee Window
(pages 64–66).

Two-Panel Lampshades and Sconces

Two-panel lampshades are relatively simple to make, as they only require the front panel to be decorated. Sconces can be made of three panels or more, allowing great flexibility in design, size, and shape. Both of these lampshade styles create a gentle, atmospheric light.

Flowering Fuchsias

The shape of this lampshade emulates the shape of the fuchsia flower. The bottom allows for a few flowers to drape over the edge, as they often do in nature. The simple pattern on the back panel increases the number of solder seams, increasing the lampshade's strength.

Materials

All of the glass in this lampshade is opalescent. It includes bright pink and purple for the flowers, various shades of green for the leaves, and a white background. You'll also need copper wire for additional support, and a vase cap.

Instructions

1 Draw a pattern for the front and back panels. See pattern on page 122 for a basic fuchsia design. Make sure the top of each panel is straight, and the same length as your vase cap.

2 Number the pieces and mark the flow of glass. Photocopy the patterns and cut out one copy of each.

3 Mark and cut the glass. Place the whole patterns on your work surface and lay the cut pieces of glass over the patterns to make sure they fit. Grind to make any adjustments and wrap the glass in copper foil. Lay the pieces for the front panel over the pattern.

4 Brush flux and tack solder key points. Turn over and tin solder the other side. Turn back over and bead solder the seams. Apply a thin layer of solder to the edges.

5 To make the back panel, lay the pieces over the back panel pattern and repeat step 4.

(continued on page 76)

A curvaceous base highlights the shape of the fuchsia flowers.

6 Wash and dry the vase cap thoroughly. Cover with flux and tin solder both sides. Take care not to touch the vase cap, as it will be very hot.

7 Use sturdy wire cutters to cut six pieces of solder. The pieces should range in length from about 2 inches to 3 inches; you'll be soldering three of them on each side of the lampshade in step 13 to hold the panels together, so make sure they are long enough to create a space between the panels that can accommodate a lightbulb.

8 Lay the vase cap upside down on your work surface. Place one of the panels against one inside edge, so that the top of the panel touches the vase cap, and the front of the panel faces outwards.

9 Tack solder the panel to the vase cap so that it is at an angle outwards. Lay the panel against a box or some other support, so that you can free your hands to hold the other panel.

10 Tack solder the other panel to the other side of the vase cap so that it rests at a similar angle, with its top touching the vase cap and the front of the panel facing outwards. At this stage, one panel is resting on a support and the other panel is being supported by your hands. It's important that you continue supporting the panels, as the weight of the glass could otherwise tear the foil.

11 With both hands, carefully turn over the lampshade so that the bottom rests on your work surface.

View of back panel.

12 Solder the pieces of cut solder on each side of the lampshade, three to each side, to hold the panels together. These will support the lampshade until step 16, when pieces of glass are soldered into place. Use a ruler to make sure both sides are even.

13 Turn over the lampshade again so that the vase cap rests on your work surface. Bead solder the inside seams connecting the panels to the vase cap. Your lampshade should be quite stable now, thanks to the strong soldering at its top and the temporary support from the pieces of solder at the sides.

14 Place a piece of paper on your work surface, lay the lampshade on its side, and trace the space between the two panels.

15 Mark and cut two pieces of glass in this shape. You can use a single piece of glass to fill the area, or make a simple pattern. Again, making a decoration increases the strength of the lampshade due to the extra solder seams. Whichever approach you take, wash and dry the glass thoroughly and wrap in copper foil.

16 Solder the glass into place, removing the six pieces of solder that have held the panels together until now as you work.

17 Apply patina. Wash well with soap and water and dry thoroughly.

View of front and side panels.

View of front panel.   *View of back and side panels.*

Bunch of Blue Flowers

*This bell-shaped lampshade casts a fair amount of light, making it perfect
for a desktop or reading corner. I used various shades of blue and green glass
to make the flowers and leaves, and white cathedral glass for the
background. The panels are made from uncolored glass cut into a flower
shape. The techniques used in this lampshade are similar to those described
in Flowering Fuchsias (pages 74–77).*

Birds on a Perch Sconce

This lovely sconce has a sense of autumn about it due to its brown, red, and green colors. The side panels contain a continuation of the composition on the main panel, allowing the branches and leaves to extend naturally.

Materials

All of the glass in this sconce is opalescent. The background is a milky white; the birds are blue and red; the branches are brown and the leaves are various shades of green. You'll also need 18-gauge copper wire to make a hook.

Instructions

1 Photocopy the patterns (pages 125–126) or draw your own pattern. If you are drawing your own pattern, I recommend making a model out of cardboard and tape to help you determine the size and angles of the panels.

2 Number the pieces and mark the flow of glass. Photocopy the patterns and cut out one of each copy.

3 Mark and cut the glass for all three panels. Wash and dry thoroughly. Place the whole patterns for all three panels on your work surface. Lay the pieces of glass on top to make sure they fit. Grind to make any adjustments, then wrap each piece in copper foil.

4 Start with the center panel. Lay the wrapped pieces of glass over the whole pattern, brush flux, and tack solder key points. Turn over and solder the other side. Turn back over and bead solder all the seams. Apply a thin layer of solder along the edges of the panel.

View of front and left panels.

View of front and right panels.

5 Repeat step 4 to make the two side panels.

6 Lay the center panel on your work surface so that the front of the panel is facing downward. Position one of the side panels to the side of the center panel so that it is at a 90° angle to the center panel and line up the seams. Make sure the front of the side panel is facing outward, and tack solder into place. Rest the panel against a box or some other support to free your hands to hold the other panel.

7 Tack solder the other side panel on the other side of the center panel in a similar manner. If you are satisfied with the angle of both panels, bead solder to secure.

8 Place the bottom of the sconce on a piece of paper and trace the space at the bottom. Mark and cut a piece of glass in this shape. Wrap in copper foil and solder into place.

9 Solder a piece of 18-gauge copper wire at the back of the sconce that extends from one side panel to the other. Solder the wire onto joints in the panels to increase its strength and make it sturdy enough for hanging the sconce.

10 Apply patina. Wash well with soap and water and dry thoroughly.

These birds at rest cast a warm, gentle light.

Bottom view of sconce.

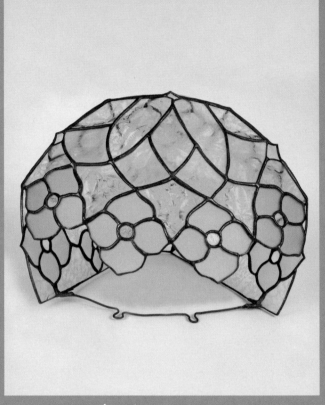

Top view of sconce.

Elegant Lace Sconce

This sconce is part of a set of light fixtures that includes the Lace Light Fixture (page 93). The sconce is constructed from five identical panels that are connected at the top with a band of flowers. This project is challenging to assemble due to the difficulty in achieving the same angle on each panel in the sconce. The techniques used in this sconce are similar to those described in Birds on a Perch Sconce (pages 79–80). See page 127 for a lace flower panel pattern.

Smiling Pansy Sconce

With their happy, mischievous faces, these little flowers
naturally come in a rainbow of colors. This makes them a
perfect subject for stained glass. The use of yellow opalescent
glass in the background conveys a warm, gentle light and
produces a calming, peaceful effect. The techniques used in this
sconce are similar to those described in Birds on a Perch Sconce
(pages 79–80).

Multi-Panel Lampshades

Panel lampshades built from three or more panels may be attached to tabletop or standing lamp bases, mounted as ceiling fixtures, or hung using a swag lamp kit. Depending upon the glass you choose, they may convey bright light suitable for reading or soft light for creating ambiance.

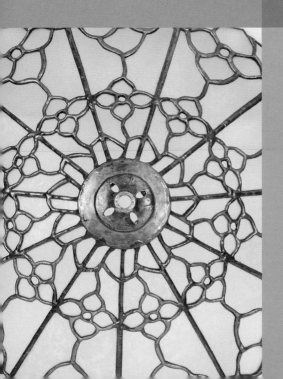

Planning in advance

Consider the lamp's final placement when designing the pattern and selecting the glass. Will it be placed in the corner of a room or hung over a table? Perhaps you are making a lampshade to suit a specific lamp base. I recommend making a model out of cardboard to determine the number and size of the panels. Here are some guidelines to keep in mind.

Panel incline

The incline of the lampshade depends upon the number of panels and their dimensions. Regarding the number of panels—the more panels in a lampshade, the less extreme the incline. For example, the incline of a three-panel lampshade is generally more severe than that of a seven-panel lampshade. Regarding the dimensions of the panels—the larger the difference between the top and the bottom of the panel, the more moderate the incline in the lampshade. For example, if the panels are perfectly rectangular, the lampshade will be perpendicular to the floor and the opening at the top and bottom of the lampshade will be the same.

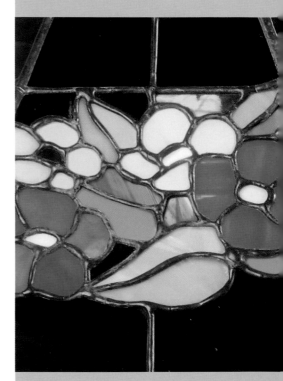

As the incline of a lampshade becomes less steep, the space at the bottom becomes wider. This affects the light projected from the lampshade. A wide bottom casts a more diffused light; a narrow bottom casts a more concentrated light.

Repetition

Multi-panel lampshades are often based on repetition. If an even number of panels is used, two different patterns can be used in alternating panels. If an uneven number of panels is used, each panel is usually identical. If the lampshade has a repeating pattern, photocopy the pattern onto a transparency and reuse to mark all of the panels. Of course, you can also make a lampshade in which each panel is different. Although this takes more planning, the result can be quite striking.

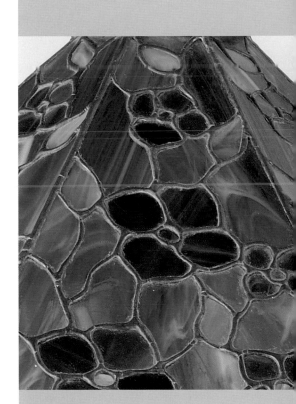

Basic Multi-Panel Lampshade

By following these steps, you can make a multi-panel lampshade with any number of panels. I recommend first making a model out of cardboard to test the number and dimensions of the panels.

Materials

The glass you choose depends upon the function and style of your design. You'll also need tape to hold the panels together temporarily, copper wire for additional support, a wooden rod, a damp cloth, and a vase cap.

Instructions

1 Assemble the lampshade panels according to your pattern, and following the basic steps for making stained glass. You can use repeated patterns on every panel, alternate between two patterns, or use different patterns for each panel. Use a jig when assembling the panels to ensure that they are all the same size. Be sure to apply a thin layer of solder along the edges of each panel after soldering the interior seams.

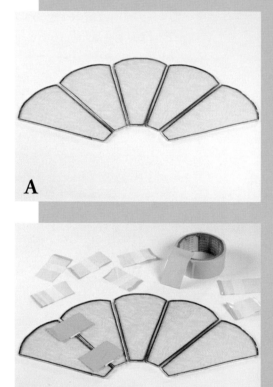

A

B

2 Lay the panels in an arc on your work surface with the front sides facing downwards (Figure A). There should be a small space between each panel, and adjoining seams should be lined up.

Tip: *It is more important for the bottom of the lampshade to be lined up than the top because this edge will be visible in the final product. The top of the lampshade will be covered by a vase cap, which will conceal any small differences between the panels.*

3 Place two pieces of tape on a pair of panels (Figure B). Take care not to put tape on solder seams, as the tape could tear the copper foil when it's removed. If you like, you can place a small piece of paper on the underside of the tape in places where it might touch the copper foil.

4 Gently pull up the pair of panels. They should touch each another gently, but shouldn't overlap, and there shouldn't be a big space between them. Return the panels to your work surface and adjust the spacing between all of the panels so that they touch gently when raised.

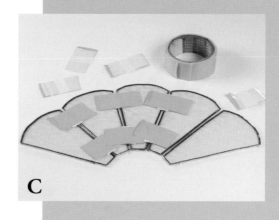

C

5 Tape all of the adjoining panels together (Figure C). Do not place tape at the top or bottom of the panels or along solder joints, as you will want to solder these areas immediately.

6 Place two pieces of tape on the last panel and allow them to hang (Figure D). You want these pieces to be handy for securing the first and last panels after drawing all of the panels up into a cone shape.

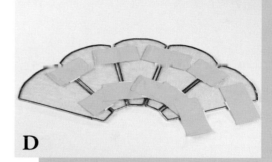

D

7 Using both hands, carefully draw up the panels by pulling the top edges of the panels upwards (Figures E1–6).

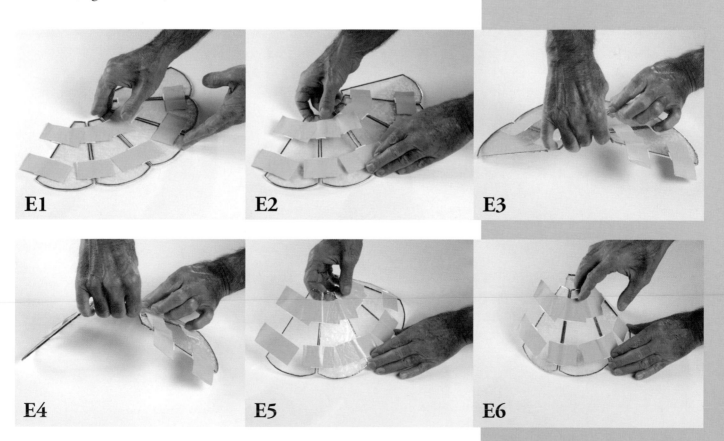

E1 **E2** **E3**

E4 **E5** **E6**

(continued on page 92)

8 When the panels are resting on their bottoms, use one hand to tape the first and last panels together (Figures G1–4).

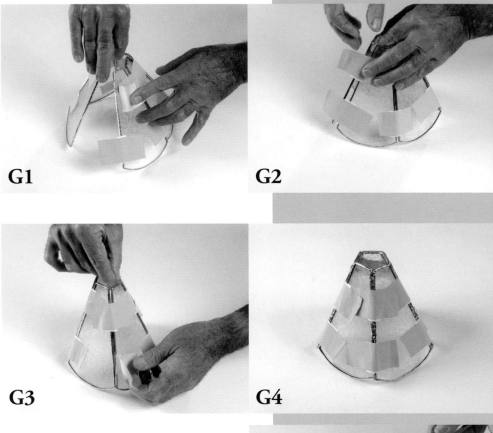

G1

G2

G3

G4

9 Tack solder the panels together in several spots, making sure to solder at the top and bottom, as well as on joints along the seams (Figure H). Apply as many dabs of solder as possible. Do not solder the taped areas.

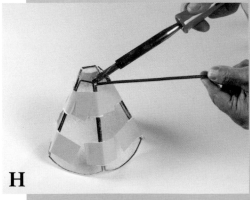

H

10 When you are sure that the solder is holding the panels together, carefully remove the tape (Figure I). Apply dabs of solder to areas that were previously covered with tape.

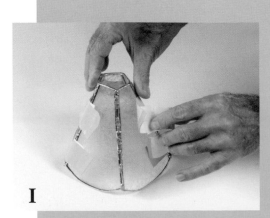

I

11 Gently lay the lampshade on a damp cloth so that it is resting on a seam between two panels. Solder the inside of the seam (Figure J). Rotate the lampshade until all the inside seams are soldered.

12 To solder the outside seams, it's best to have both hands free. To do this, I recommend making a support by wrapping a wooden rod in a damp cloth and propping up the rod with two small boxes so that it is parallel to the floor. Place the lampshade over the rod and bead solder the seams between the panels (Figure K). Rotate the lampshade until all the outside seams are soldered.

13 Place the lampshade so that the top is on your work surface and the bottom is facing upwards. Solder a piece of copper wire along the bottom edge for additional support.

14 Wash and dry the vase cap thoroughly. Cover with flux and tin solder both sides. Take care not to touch the vase cap as you solder, as it will be very hot.

15 Place the lampshade so that the bottom is on your work surface and the top is facing upwards. Center the vase cap over the top and tack solder into place. Bead solder to finish.

16 Apply patina. Wash well with soap and water and dry thoroughly.

Tip: When assembling panel lampshades, there are two stages when one can attach the vase cap. I prefer soldering it on after the lampshade has been fully soldered, but you can also solder it on when the panels are still held in place with tape. Attaching the vase cap at this point adds to the lampshade's stability; however, it also limits your access to the inside seams of the lampshade, making it impossible to use a rod to support the lampshade as you solder the outside seams. Experience is the best way of determining which method is best for you.

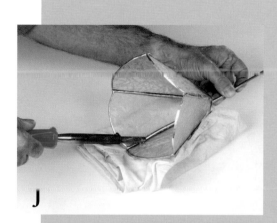

J

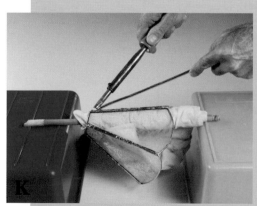

K

Flowers on Brown Lampshade

This lampshade is suited to a corner that doesn't require a lot of light, as the dark brown background emits a soft, gentle glow. The colorful flowers burst out of the brown, creating a lovely and lively contrast. The techniques used in this lampshade are similar to those described in
Basic Multi-Panel Lampshade (pages 88–91).

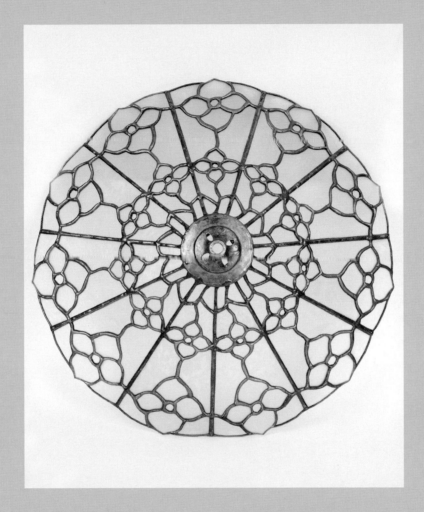

Lace Light Fixture

This lampshade has a relatively mild incline due to the large
number of panels. It includes uncolored glass and transmits a
lot of light, making it perfect as a ceiling fixture.
The techniques used in this lampshade are similar to those
described in Basic Multi-Panel Lampshade (pages 88–91).

Purple Lace Lampshade

*This lampshade has only seven panels, resulting in a medium
inclination and making it perfect for a desk or standing lamp.
The use of various shades of purple and green opalescent glass
creates a subdued, mellow light. The techniques used in this
lampshade are similar to those described in
Basic Multi-Panel Lampshade (pages 88–91).*

Transparent Lace Lampshade

This lampshade has only seven panels, resulting in a medium inclination and making it perfect for a desk or standing lamp. The use of transparent glass allows it to convey a considerable amount of light. The techniques used in this lampshade are similar to those described in Basic Multi-Panel Lampshade (pages 88–91).

Domed Lampshades

The technique for making domed lampshades is rarely described in craft books because these lampshades are usually based on molds that come with their own specifications and measurements. The technique described below is adaptable to any rounded mold, allowing you endless opportunities for creative expression.

Planning in advance

Domed lampshades are immensely flexible, as they involve a continuous flow of images that never repeats itself. The technique requires a lot of improvisation, so make sure you are very comfortable working with stained glass before you begin.

Choosing the mold

Designing your domed lampshade begins with the shape of your mold. You can buy molds at hobby stores or online; you can also use objects you have lying around your home such as round light fixtures or large bowls. Keep your eyes open for any object with a shape that appeals to you; you'll be surprised at what you may find!

Design

Choose images for your lampshade using sources such as stained glass journals, magazines, and the Internet. For your first project, I recommend choosing subjects with templates such as birds, flowers, or animals. The lampshade is made in stages, so choose primary and secondary elements for your design. You'll arrange the primary elements first, adapting the secondary elements and background afterwards so that they integrate nicely.

Large bowls, light fixtures, and other round objects can serve as molds for this technique.

Field of Poppies

The red and black poppies in this lampshade add a burst of brilliance to any living room or study. Bright red poppies are accompanied by yellow and white wildflowers, and green stems and leaves. This project brings a lovely sense of the outdoors inside.

Materials

This lampshade uses several bright colors of glass; it's an excellent design for using leftover pieces of glass in any shade. You'll also need copper wire and a vase cap.

Instructions

1 Choose a plastic bowl or mold that is the size and shape of the desired lampshade.

2 Draw a general sketch of the lampshade, then draw patterns for the primary elements. There is no need for repetition, so feel free to make each element distinct. Also, remember that the exact dimensions of the secondary elements and the background will only be determined after the primary elements have been soldered into place.

3 Number the pieces and mark the flow of glass. Photocopy the patterns and cut out one copy. Place the whole patterns on your work surface.

4 Mark and cut the glass. Use sturdy wire cutters to cut several 6-inch pieces of solder. You'll need these pieces to temporarily support the elements on the mold, so make sure you have many pieces on hand.

(continued on page 102)

This wooden lamp base includes delicately engraved leaves and flowers.

5 Lay the pieces for one poppy at a time on your work surface so that the side that will face the inside of the lampshade is facing upwards. Brush flux and lightly tack solder key points. This solder will act as hinges when the pieces are shaped onto the mold.

Tip: If you apply too much solder in step 5 the pieces of glass won't conform to the shape of the mold. Remove solder by heating it with the solder iron and allowing it to gently come away from the glass. Don't try to pull the pieces apart, as this will simply rip the copper foil.

6 Repeat step 5 until all the poppies are assembled.

7 Solder a 6-inch piece of solder onto an upper joint of one poppy. Position the poppy onto the mold so that the soldered side is touching the mold, and gently bend the poppy so that it takes on the shape of the mold. Heat the piece of solder and bend it over the top of the mold and onto the other side to provide a counterweight to support the poppy.

Tip: These poppies are quite small, so it is fairly easy to transfer them onto the mold. If you are making a lampshade with larger primary elements, tack soldering may not be strong enough to support the whole element as you transfer it to the mold. In such cases, assemble the primary elements in sections, and solder the sections together directly on the mold.

8 Repeat step 7 until all of the poppies are on the mold. You can also solder pieces of solder between the poppies to hold them in place; just remember that having too many pieces of solder on the mold may interfere in your work.

9 After all the poppies have been arranged, adjust their position and curvature so that they rest smoothly against the mold. Tin solder all of the seams.

10 Now that the primary elements of your lampshade have been soldered into place, you can prepare the secondary elements; in this case, the flowers and stems. Lay a transparency onto the mold and draw basic outlines for these elements.

11 Mark and cut the glass for each element. Wrap in foil and arrange directly onto the mold, soldering them to pieces of solder, poppies, or each other. At this stage, you will have a network of primary and secondary elements on the mold, held together by pieces of solder. As you fill in more spaces with glass, remove the pieces of solder.

12 Mark the top border of your lampshade according to the size of your vase cap. As for the bottom border, you can mark a straight border or allow the border to accommodate the natural shape of the elements.

13 Once all secondary elements are in place, make the background by filling in the gaps. If you are using cathedral glass, place the glass over the gap and trace the shape directly onto the glass. If the background is opalescent, trace the gap onto a transparency and then mark the glass. Cut, wrap, and solder the background pieces into place.

Tip: Filling a large gap with a single piece of glass may distort the curvature of the lampshade. In such cases, I recommend using several pieces of glass to fill the gap. Solder the pieces onto the mold one at a time so that they conform to the shape of the mold.

14 After the background has been filled, solder the outside seams of the lampshade. When the lampshade is stable, remove it from the mold and place upside down on a damp cloth, so that the inside of the lampshade faces upwards. Solder the inside seams of the lampshade, rotating it as you work.

15 Solder a piece of copper wire along the bottom edge of the lampshade for additional support.

16 Place a damp cloth on the inside of the lampshade and turn it over onto the mold again, so that the cloth is flush against the interior of the lampshade. If the lampshade doesn't fit onto the mold because of the seams, place it right side up on your work surface and use one hand to hold a damp cloth against the inside seams. Use the other hand to bead solder the exterior of the lampshade.

17 Wash and dry the vase cap thoroughly. Cover with flux and tin solder both sides. Take care not to touch the vase cap, as it will be very hot. When cool, solder the vase cap into place.

18 Apply patina. Wash well with soap and water and dry thoroughly.

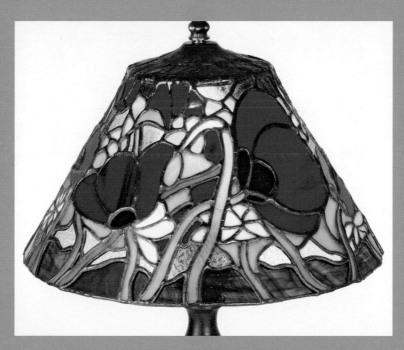

Close view of red poppies, white wildflowers, and green stems.

Full view of lampshade and base.

Top view of lampshade.

Harvest Season in the Vineyard

The main challenge in this lampshade was making each bunch of grapes look distinct and authentic. The first elements I soldered onto the lampshade were the branches that dominate the upper quarter of the lampshade. These formed the base onto which I built the grapes and the leaves. I sketched several different styles of grape clusters first, then assembled them separately on my work surface using purple nuggets. I tack soldered the leaves first, then soldered each nugget according to the pattern.

The techniques used in this lampshade are similar to those described in Field of Poppies (pages 100–104).

Full view of lampshade and base.   Top view of lampshade.

Birds in a Magnolia Tree

Birds in flight are naturally distinct, making them perfect subjects for this
style of lampshade. The secondary elements are flowers, leaves, and branches,
all of which are highly flexible subjects, and conducive to the natural curves
of the lampshade. The colorless background sets off the birds and flowers and
allows the lampshade to convey a bright, illuminating light.
The techniques used in this lampshade are similar to those described in Field
of Poppies (pages 100–104).

Full view of lampshade and base.　　　　　　*Top view of lampshade.*

Gathering of Goldfinches

*The primary elements in this lampshade are birds, in several poses and a
plethora of colors. I referred to nature magazines and stained glass journals
for sketches of birds, adapting the designs to suit my mold.
The techniques used in this lampshade are similar to those described in
Field of Poppies (pages 100–104).*

Full view of lampshade and base.

Top view of lampshade.

India Experience

This project was inspired by several months I spent traveling with my wife
in India. The colors, textures, wildlife, and landscape of the region left a
great impression on my imagination. The addition of small mirrors was
inspired by the use of small mirrors in Indian clothing and decorations.
The techniques used in this lampshade are similar to those described in Field
of Poppies (pages 100–104).

Patterns

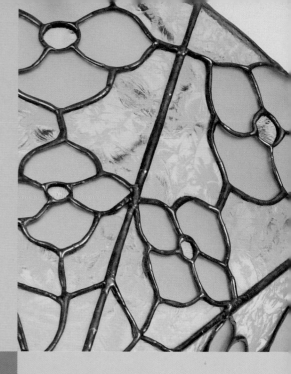

The following pages contain patterns for several projects described in this book. Trace or photocopy, and enlarge to the desired size. Also, feel free to adjust any pattern by adding or removing details.

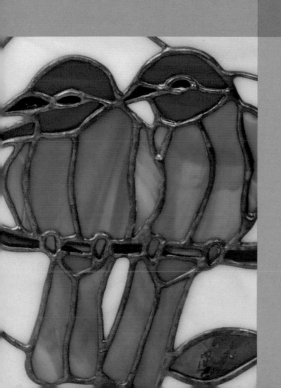

Butterfly at Rest (100%)

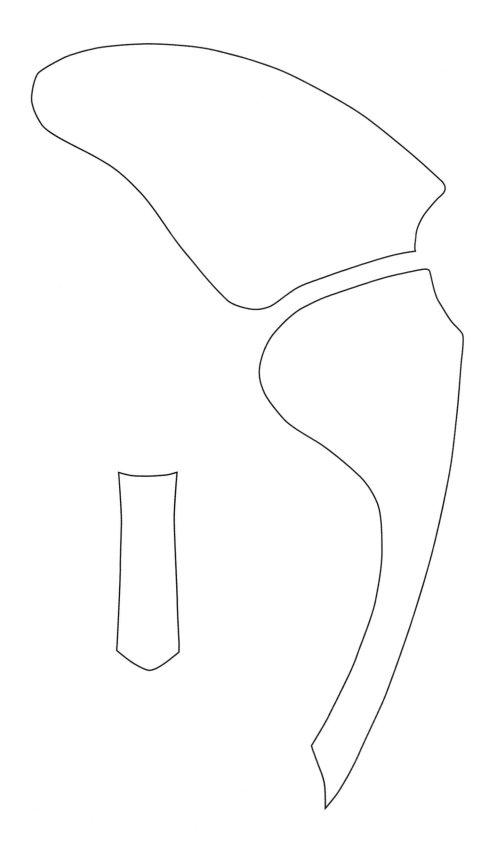

Crab

Turtle

Dolphin

Decorated Glass Vessel (100%)

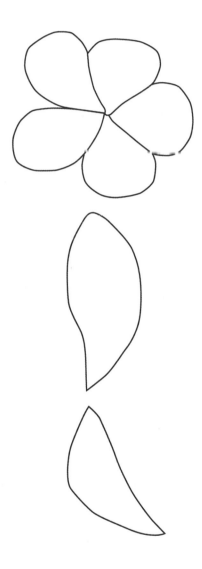

Three-Petal Coaster (100%)

Butterfly—Ready for Flight (100%)

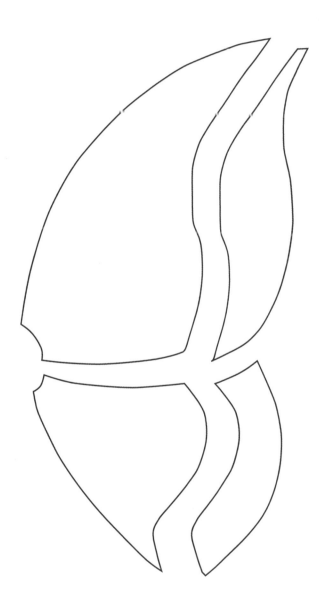

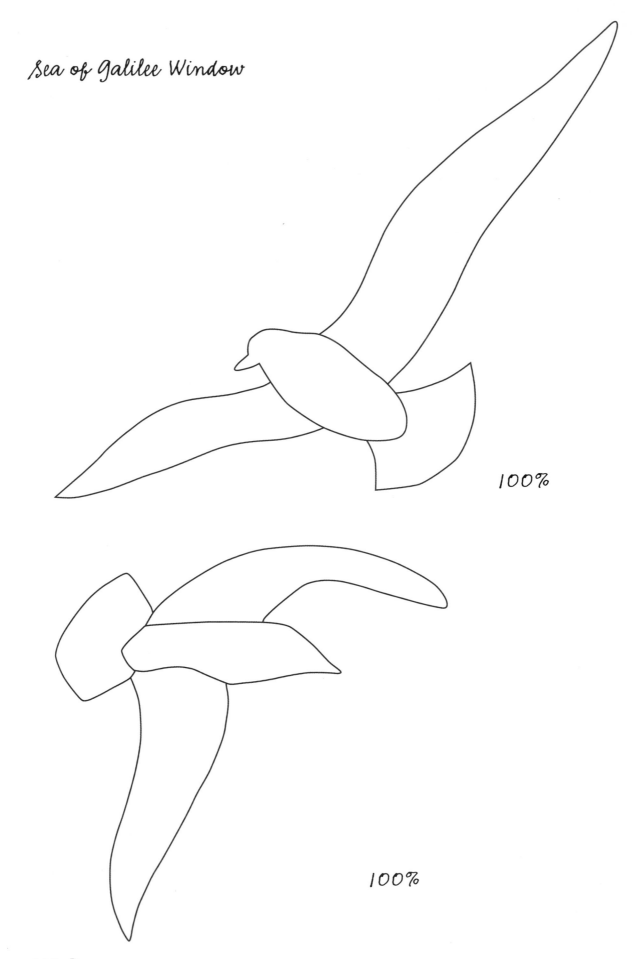

100%

100%

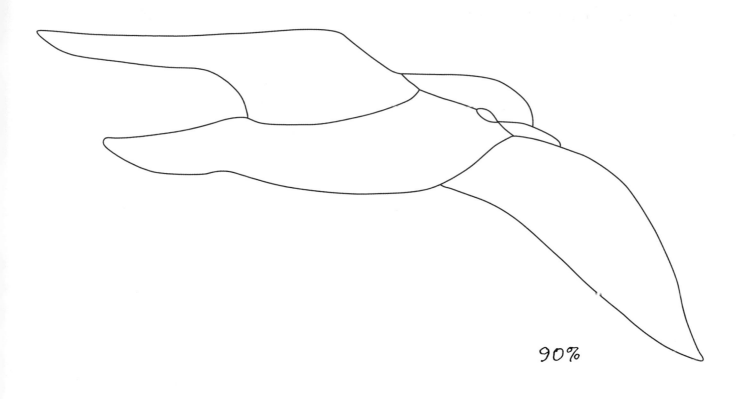

90%

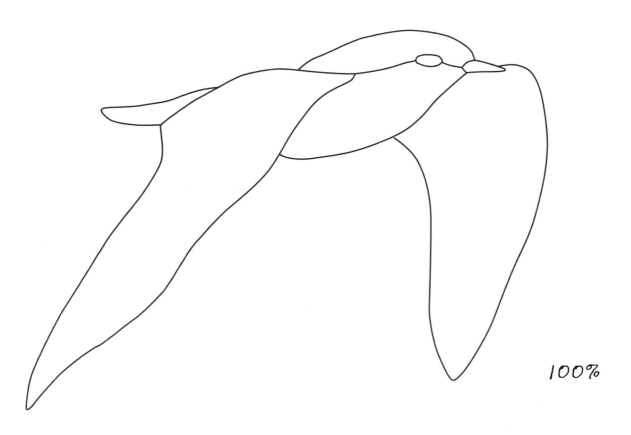

100%

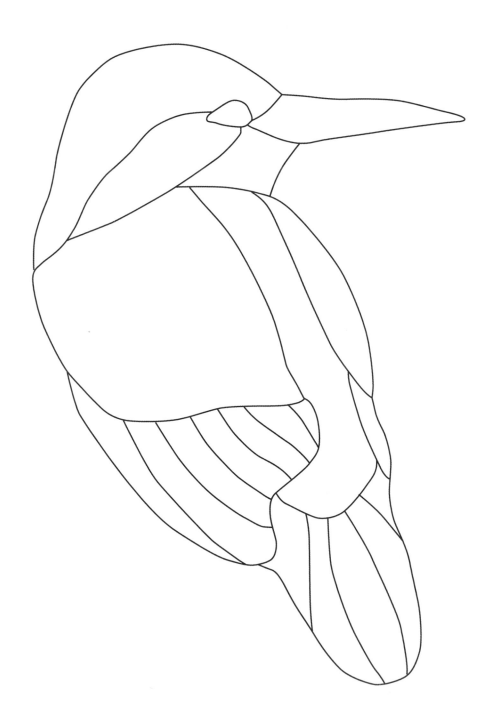

100%

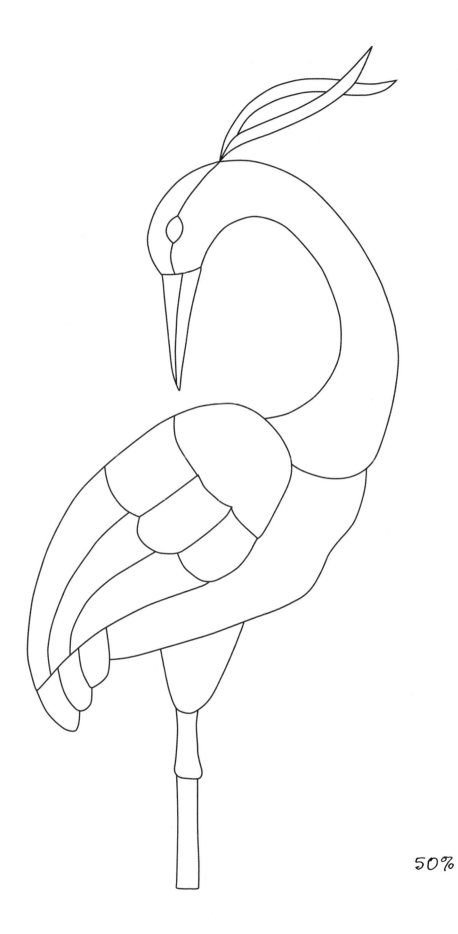

50%

Four Fuchsia Windows (80%)

Purple Lace Windows (60%)

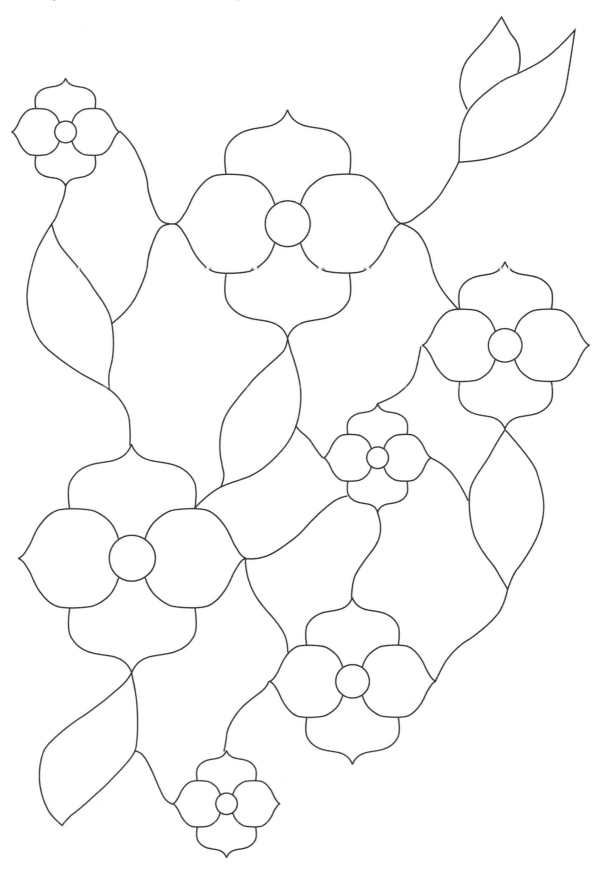

Indigo Morning Glory Window (65%)

Birds on a Perch Sconce (80%)

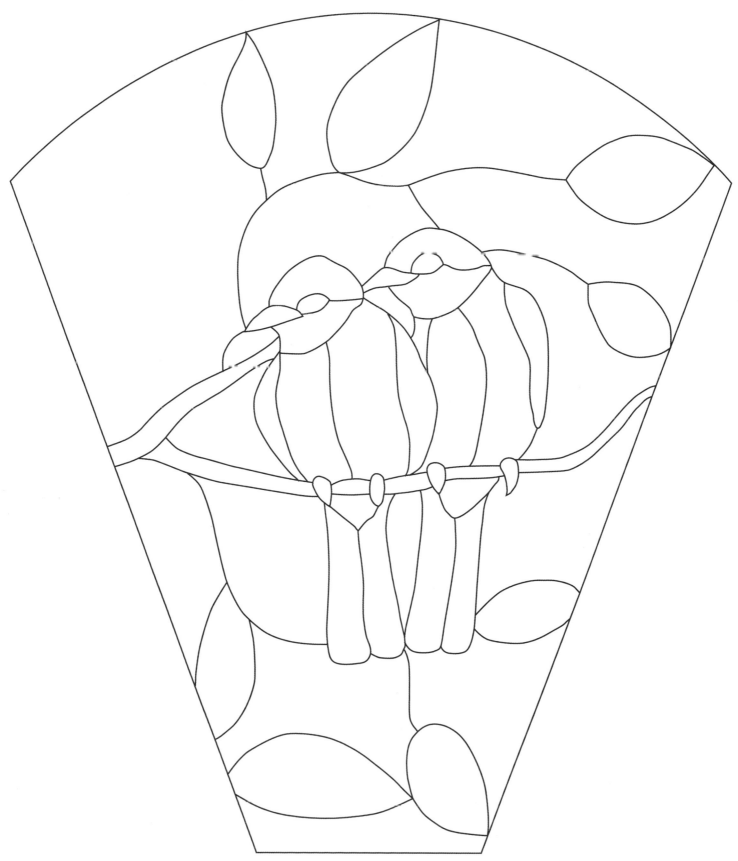

Birds on a Perch Sconce (80%)

left

right

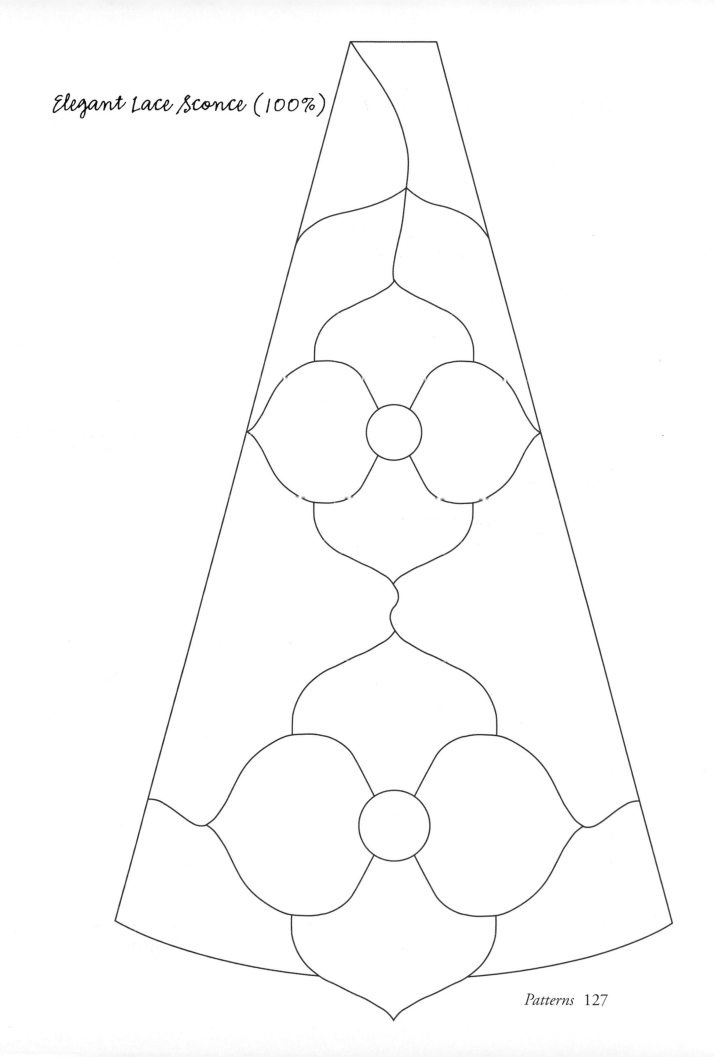

Elegant Lace Sconce (100%)

Index

Metric Equivalents					
inches	cm	inches	cm	inches	cm
1	2.54	11	27.94	21	53.34
2	5.08	12	30.48	22	55.88
3	7.62	13	33.02	23	58.42
4	10.16	14	35.56	24	60.96
5	12.7	15	38.1	30	76.2
6	15.24	16	40.64	36	91.44
7	17.78	17	43.18	42	106.68
8	20.32	18	45.72	48	121.92
9	22.86	19	48.26	54	137.16
10	25.4	20	50.8	60	152.4